THE LEANER ADVANTAGE

A Quick-Hit Guide to Fortune 500 Process Improvement Methodologies for Businesses, both Big and Small

IVAN G. BANNOWSKY

DEDICATION

For my grandfather, Commander Clarence James Bannowsky, Jr., U.S. Navy (Retired), Pilot, WWII Hero and Purple Heart Recipient, who, even at the age of 100 years old, continued to inspire me in life and never ceased to encourage me to complete this work.

"Oh, I have slipped the surly bonds of earth,
And danced the skies on laughter-silvered wings;
Sunward I've climbed and joined the tumbling mirth of sun-split
clouds - and done a hundred things You have not dreamed of -
wheeled and soared and swung high in the sunlit silence.
Hovering there I've chased the shouting wind along
and flung my eager craft through footless halls of air.

"Up, up the long delirious burning blue
I've topped the wind-swept heights with easy grace,
where never lark, or even eagle, flew;
and, while with silent, lifting mind I've trod
the high untrespassed sanctity of space,
put out my hand and touched the face of God."

- "High Flight" by John McGee, Jr.

.

CONTENTS

ACKNOWLEDGMENTS

To my family, friends, and colleagues over the years, thank you for being generous with the knowledge.

PREFACE

Small businesses are the backbone of the American economy and according to the Small Business Administration they account for almost half of the private non-farm GDP. It goes without saying that owning and/or operating a small business in the United States is part of the American Dream, a dream founded on the principles of hard work, industriousness, and self-motivation.

While there are many resources available to the entrepreneur, in many cases there is barely enough time in the day to dedicate to anything other than ensuring that the business is running, much less that it is running *efficiently*. This is the challenge at hand. Efficiency is defined as achieving maximum productivity with minimum wasted effort or expense. What efficiency is not, is simply being able to produce more product faster. The aim of Process Improvement is not to reduce the number of employees, but rather to reduce cycle times and risk. Many highly successful companies make it a top priority to retain employees in order to preserve the knowledge and experience required for the entity to be successful and sustainable.

The United States has one of the lowest Labor Productivity rates among developed and industrialized nations in the world. I venture to say that this does not stem from a culture of laziness, but rather from a disengaged workforce frustrated with inefficient processes. Within each of my careers in varying industries I have observed complacency with the status quo and an unwillingness to invest a little time now to reap huge rewards later. When I was introduced to Continuous Process Improvements Methodologies such as Six Sigma, LEAN and Business Process Management, I resisted at first; however, after sinking my teeth into them and witnessing firsthand the practical application and the successes that were achieved, I was in.

Seasoned Process Improvement practitioners familiar with these mainstream methodologies will surely notice the DMAIC Framework of Define, Measure, Analyze, Improve, and Control in this work; however the intent here is to streamline and simplify these into more easily digested morsels of information. I do not imply that these tools are cookie cutter and that all the examples will fit your business. You will need to identify how best to apply them and leverage some creativity for optimum success. Also, this is not an attempt to describe any one process improvement methodology and is most certainly not intended to minimize the effectiveness of others. So, for you Purists out there, don't be alarmed; this book is intended to provide low hanging fruit for novices of process improvement as well as a fresh perspective for those that are well versed.

I do recommend that you read this book in its entirety, which should be easy due to its brevity; however, you may find you do not need all of the tools. Extract what's applicable to you and keep the book close for reference. To quote Albert Einstein, "Never memorize something that you can lookup." Utilizing this book alone will not make you an expert at Process Improvement, but you will get enough to benefit your business. You can certainly gain further benefit by continuing to research these methodologies as you delve deeper into your journey.

It wasn't until I witnessed the inner workings of a pizza shop did I realize that these Process Improvement Methodologies typically leveraged solely by Fortune 500 companies were sorely missed at the Small Business level. It was then I decided to embark on the endeavor of making this knowledge accessible and relevant to Main Street by writing this book. I opted to use examples of a Pizza Shop throughout the book, as I believe it is relatable and easily transferable to any business. You will find parallels in production and customer-facing interaction, including internal customers to whom you deliver product and services within the entity, and external customers whom are acquired through marketing, walk-ins, and other means as well as third party vendors. Additionally, customer service should not stop with your clients. It should also be applied with colleagues within the organization. You may also see me use examples of an imaginary product called 'widgets.' This is a term commonly used for illustrative purposes in industry as a variable to any given company's product..

I have written this book in the spirit of a quick read designed to give you the most 'bang for your buck.' While the title is "The Leaner Advantage, A Quick-Hit Guide to Process Improvement for Businesses, Both Big and Small," those involved with the Process Improvement behemoths inside of major corporations can benefit from reading this as well as those seeking an introduction to process improvement. Well-intentioned operations can sometimes be self-defeating when they over-complicate the very process of Process Improvement and lose sight of what is important. Thus, I have also strived to make the tools easy to implement. After all, you have a business to run.

As opposed to creating an avalanche of tools that are used in large projects by conglomerates, I have prioritized speed to market, which smaller organizations need, and quick hits that will be easy to put into play. I avoid techniques that require extended periods of time to complete and mountains of resources, such as finances and manpower, that only large firms have readily at their disposal. These methodologies can be applied to a plethora of sectors including manufacture, service, marketing, acquisitions, hiring, building, sales, non-profit logistics and general operations; all with the intent of making your entity sustainable and developing your most valuable asset; your workforce.

This book is not solely about Process Improvement and Risk Mitigation. Where applicable, I have included certain nuggets of business knowledge that you can also apply to your organization. It is my hope that you, the reader, business owner, manager, or entrepreneur can apply the concepts that I lay out here before you and that you achieve the successes that you seek on you way to capturing the American Dream.

Lastly, I've included a chapter on motivation, because I believe it is necessary to recognize the importance of developing this trait, not only to ensure that we take action to improve our processes, but also because it is something I have seen, and recognized with myself personally; that is lacking in today's society. Having struggled with procrastination and moments of less than desirable levels of motivation, I share with you helpful strategies for self-motivation and attaining a fulfilling and happy life. A little motivation to start your process improvement journey.

1

WHY IMPROVE?

"Perfection is not attainable, but if we chase perfection we can catch excellence"

- Vince Lombardi

Why improve? Great question, and one that is not asked often enough. Why should you try to improve your process or business? The answer is simple; the bottom line. Follow the money. The green in that lean green machine is cash. All roads lead to the primary indicator of your business' success, which is how far away you can stay away from the red. Not only that, but as a Small Business Owner or Manger, you know that the business's success is tied closely to your own personal success and that of the employees. We all seek a sense of accomplishment, and running a businesses that is well-managed is key to this end. Morale plummets when things are bumpy, and it makes it exponentially difficult to pull things back up again. Families and quality of life are dependent on the business.

The old adage of "If your business isn't growing, it's dying" may ring true; however, I prefer to focus more on "If your business isn't improving its processes, than it's not going to grow the right way." While common Business Plan templates, such as those provided by the Small Business Administration, do not include initiatives of process improvement, they should be an integral part of your overall plan. In other terms, innovation should always trump stagnation.

Improving isn't just about making the process or the business as a whole more efficient, it is also about Risk Mitigation which is defined as a systemic reduction of exposure and occurrence of risk. No doubt you already perform this within your operation, be it by stocking newer perishable items in the back of the rotation so that items expiring sooner will move off the shelves first or compliance with Standards set by the Occupational Safety and Health Administration (OSHA), so that you can keep your employees safe. The ability for you to identify where breakdowns can occur, not just those that stop production, but those that can cost in other ways is equally, if not more, important to identify than opportunities to make your process work 'better.'

Risk includes anything that can cost money or harm, be it litigation, negligence, regulatory infractions, or personal safety. If you are in a highly regulated industry, which is just about everything these days, it is imperative that you practice

Process Improvement and Risk Mitigation, lest your business close shop no sooner than it opens. Above all, risk of personal injury should be the first and foremost priority for all businesses. People should *always* come first and not just as it pertains to potential bodily harm, but as you will see in the following chapters, it is people, like the customers and the employees that operate the business, that make or break the venture, so it is imperative to pay extra special attention to them.

Employees get frustrated with processes that are inefficient or are designed poorly, and they know one when they see it. In many cases, they feel it is not their place or that their opinion would not be welcome, so they say nothing. Your most valuable assets for improving your process or business will be the performers of it. They are closest and most intimate with the tasks and you would be wise to get their input.

A primary reason for high turnover is that employees think their jobs are too hard and that management won't listen to their ideas to make them easier and more efficient. Let employees be part of the solution and you'll retain them longer and your costs for hiring and training new employees will go down. Successful businesses develop all of their employees to be leaders, not just those that are people managers. Before beginning any Process Improvement initiative, be sure to discuss your vision with the team so they understand what the objective is. They will appreciate the inclusion and you will have their buy-in to be engaged in the success of the initiative.

While these methodologies are a great way to improve your business, be wary of getting bogged down and too far into the weeds with overzealous initiatives. It will be necessary to find a balance between thoroughness and speed to market, ensuring that you are getting sufficient value for the investment of effort. In any business, one assumes a certain tolerance of risk, and while we can attempt to instill controls to guard against these risks the business operates at this level, lest it should paint itself into a corner and cannot function.

Don't be surprised if by the end of this book you find yourself identifying opportunities to improve processes wherever you encounter them. Whether it's the grocery store, your own garage or sitting in a long line at a toll gate, processes are everywhere. Take the opportunity to observe the world around you, and I guarantee you can pick up ideas to apply to your own business. Why reinvent the wheel, right?

Lastly, if nothing else, it is in the spirit of industriousness and inventiveness that should compel us to constantly seek better ways to do what we do. If not for human inquisitiveness we would still be in the Stone Age, so it is almost a birthright, nay, an obligation that we aim to create better tools to enhance our lives in a responsible fashion. It is indeed; our legacy that we pass to the next generation a better world than the one that was handed to us and this, dear reader, is achievable, in part, with the tools presented in the following chapters of this book.

The visual below, *Fig. A*, is one example of the building blocks of a business. At the top priority we find People, consisting of Customers and Employees (including Owners and Managers). The foundation is comprised of the Process, the Product, and the Business as a whole.

Fig. A

The Building Blocks of a Business

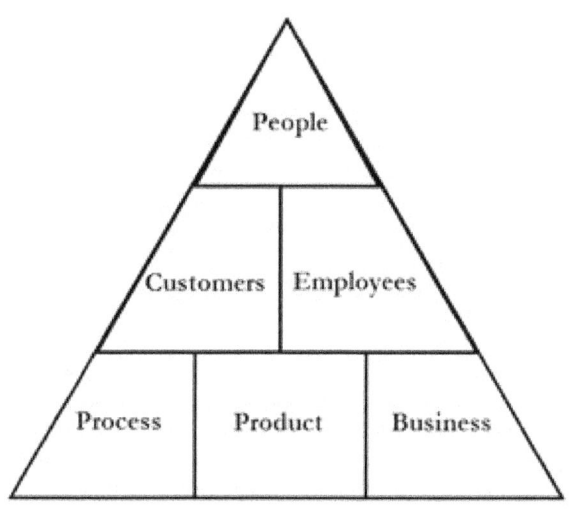

IVAN G. BANNOWSKY

2

KNOW THY CUSTOMER

"The Customer is Always Right"

- Harry Gordon Selfridge, Founder

Selfridge's Department Store

London, 1909

Human interaction has involved the bartering of services and goods for millennia, and since the beginning, the customer has had the power to either accept or refuse the deal based on their need or want. Not much has changed in this respect as this still rings true today. Understanding what satisfies customers is key to any entity's survival, be it negotiating across a fruit vendor's stand or at the high-rise boardroom table. Innovators know all too well that the next product they develop must fill a gap in our daily lives; otherwise, it will quickly die on the vine.

Customers typically want a product that is high in quality, they want it fast, and they want it cheap. Quite often they want all of this at the same time with little room for compromise. Companies constantly scramble to deliver these and many often miss the mark because they have not taken the time or effort to find out what really matters to their customers. They usually produce what *they* consider to be of high quality, at acceptable speed, and at a good price. They then expect the customer to conform to their notion and not the other way around. Broad assumptions are made with the justification that they have placed themselves in the customer's shoes and that therefore their perspectives are equal to that of the true target customer. Usually, not enough is done to actually survey the customer and identify what it is that they are looking for in the product, how quickly they need it and what they are willing to pay for it. Paradoxically, this may also mean that you may need to try to know what your customers' wants and needs are even before they do. Be ready; however, to adapt once these should shift or are more clearly identified.

Knowing your customers' wants can be achieved through trial and error as well as going out on a limb to try new variations of your product and/or services. The customer is indeed the foundation for the very existence of the business, and if we are not listening to them then failure is inevitable. While there are many ways to survey customers, be it email, websites, or other electronic media, do not hesitate to get out onto the street, with a clipboard in hand if needed, and specifically survey your customers face to face. What better way to get to know your potential customers than to go out and meet them and survey their expectations instead of waiting for them to come to you? It's also a great way to drum up business. They will surely appreciate the effort made to understand their needs.

Fig. B gives an example of what a Pizza Shop Owner's Survey could look like that seeks to identify what his or her potential customers' needs and wants might be.

Fig. B

Pizza Shop Survey

Date:_____ Location: Main St. Survey #: _____

1) What is most important to you when ordering a pizza?

a) Taste   b) Price   c) Speed   d)Other_____

2) What is the most important factor in the taste of the pizza?

a) Cheese   b) Crust   c) Sauce   d) Spices

3) For a delivery, how fast do you expect your pizza to arrive?

a) 15 mins   b) 25 mins   c) 35 mins   d) 45 mins

4) How much are you willing to pay for a good Large Cheese Pizza?

a) $6.99   b) $8.99   c) $10.99   d) $12.99

IVAN G. BANNOWSKY

You can tailor your survey to your product/service and target what it is you really need to find out from customers. Once you have your surveys, it is ideal to input the data into a spreadsheet so that you can tally and identify what your customers want. I won't go into how many surveys you should collect in order to obtain a good understanding of your customer base that would be statistically viable. I will say that once you begin to see a trend emerge anecdotally, I recommend continuing to gather additional data from surveying until you can ensure that there is a clear leader in your results. *Fig. C* is an example of a spreadsheet where data is collected and the results tallied from the survey.

Fig. C   Survey Results

What is most important to you when ordering a pizza?	a) Taste	b) Price	c) Speed	d)Other
	18	27	35	N/A
What is the most important factor in the taste of the pizza?	a) Cheese	b) Crust	c) Sauce	d) Spices
	7	31	39	3
For a delivery, how fast do you expect your pizza to arrive?	a) 15 mins	b) 25 mins	c) 35 mins	d) 45 mins
	3	24	52	1
How much are you willing to pay for a Large Cheese Pizza?	a) $6.99	b) $8.99	c) $10.99	d) $12.99
	14	25	29	12

You may want to also place your data into a graph, depending on the complexity of your survey and the results. Below, in *Fig. D.* is an example of taking the data from the Price question on the survey to see where the majority of the answers fall.

Fig. D

Survey Results Graph

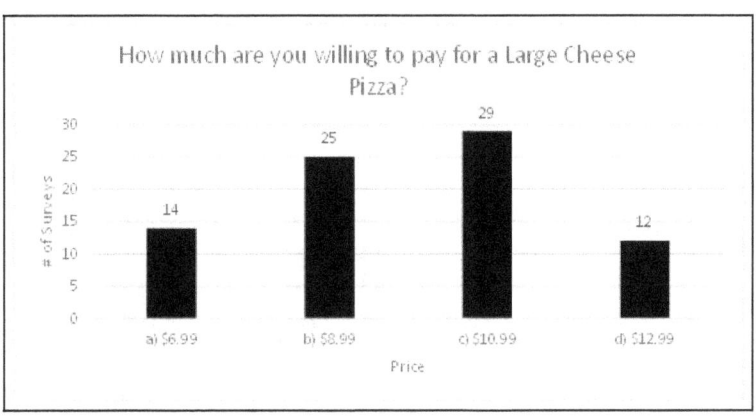

As you can see, the majority of the customers answered around the $8.99-$10.99 range. One could surmise that the ideal pricing for the pizza would be around $9.99. This is, of course, only if it allows for a sufficient profit margin. If you find that whatever your customers are surveying out at and what you can reasonably price or operate your business at are really far away from each other, then it will be time to revisit your survey and ensure that it is asking the right questions and that your capabilities are properly assessed.

Fig. E

Customer Survey Map

Pizza Shop Customer's Expectation:

"I expect my pizza to be delicious, hot, fast and reasonbly priced."

Category	Qualifier	Goal	Priority
Quality	Hot	Between 150° F and 170° F	Medium
	Delicious	Customer says Yum!	High
Speed	Pick-up	Less than 15 minutes	Medium
	Delivery	Less than 35 minutes	Medium
Price	Cheese	$10.99	Medium
	Pepporoni	$12.99	High
	Meat Lover's	$16.99	High

On the opposing page, the Customer Survey Map, *Fig. E*, shows that our pizza place customers expect their pizza to be delicious, hot, fast, and reasonably priced. This maps what is important to the customer to build your business' base, keep 'em coming back, and establish specific goals to make this possible. You can use Excel or Visio to create this.

In the Customer Survey Map, you will want to identify a statement that the customer would make if they were to communicate to you what it is specifically that is their expectation. In this case, it would be "I expect my pizza to be delicious, hot, fast and reasonably priced." This will provide you with a tangible voice of the customer instead of 'cold' numbers or a desensitized corporate statement. Next, you will want to create a Category column where you will list what types of metrics you are looking to target. Typically, these will be Quality, Speed, and Price. You may identify other categories depending upon your business needs. Examples of these could be Internal Costs, Compliance, and Employee Morale. Next, you will want to identify the qualifiers that are being targeted within the Categories. In other words, specifics regarding your categories and their makeup. In this example, qualifiers for the category of Quality are Hot and Delicious; Speed is for either Pick-up or Delivery; and Price is contingent on the Toppings desired. The Goal column will be the target measurement that will satisfy the customer's requirement and, lastly, the Priority column will assist in identifying where you should concentrate your efforts, time, and resources according to the level of importance it has for the customer and the business.

You may find that you want to do several of these customer survey maps for your organization depending on how complex your products, services and business are. Use your judgment on what makes sense in terms of scope. For example, you may want to do a separate survey for each of your products contingent how different they are from each other. I do not recommend you try to do just one that contains excessive information that the unwitting reviewer cannot absorb within a few moments. This would be counterproductive. It should be easily digestible for anyone that picks it up to look for review and should only require minimal explanation from its creator. Otherwise, this lends to a muddled message and you and your team will miss out on the value of the tool. Examples of other categories for the Pizza Shop could be 'Ingredient Freshness' and 'Order Accuracy.' I recommend you revisit you Customer Survey Map(s) once a month or, at the very least, quarterly to ensure you still have your customer' profiles captured accurately. Finally, understand that product and process are not mutually exclusive. Just because you are not changing the 'ingredients' of your product, you can still drive quality and speed through the actual process by which you produce the product. You could have the best ingredients or raw materials in the world; however. if you are not mixing them or putting them together in a way that drives quality, speed, and price, you might as well be working with the worst materials in the world. One could argue that you could use substandard ingredients in a 'best in class' process and produce a superior product than the reverse. Not surprisingly, this is often the case.

Keep in mind that the success of your business is directly tied to customer satisfaction. Keep them happy and they will keep coming back. If you do not keep them happy then you will soon see the business struggling to survive with a dwindling clientele. The relationship between business and customer is a microcosm of dependency. Each needs the other to exist. While the business may set its own goals on what it wants to achieve, these should not stray far from what the customer is looking for too.

IVAN G. BANNOWSKY

3

DOCUMENTATION

"Ink is better than the best memory."

- Chinese Proverb

If you do not already have your processes documented, then it is imperative that this be one of your first steps on the road to process improvement. These are commonly known as manuals, procedures, policies, work instructions, step-by-steps, protocols, SOPs (Standard Operating Procedures), or anything else where the processes are documented. I highly recommend, if you do not have these written already, to do so now, even if it means putting your process improvement efforts on hold. It is not advisable to attempt to improve your processes with the tools laid out in this book while you are trying to document them at the same time. Attempting to document your process and improve them in tandem can cause the Endless Loop Syndrome, where you are constantly re-working the document. Leave the improvement piece until after you've documented your processes as is. If nothing else, you should have your procedures documented already as part of normal operations, long before attempting improvements.

When writing your procedures, keep in mind that you most likely know the process well and will make assumptions about what does or doesn't need to be written. These documented procedures should be used for training new employees and will need more details to understand the process than you may initially assume. This will be an exercise in taking what is called Passive Knowledge; a shorthand on how to perform the process known commonly by only a few, into what is called Explicit Knowledge; that which is documented and can be shared by all.

In other words, you may have some real experts that have been doing the process for a long time and know all the ins, outs, and nuances. When the need to train someone else on the process arises; the transference of all of the knowledge and experience of the expert is less likely to occur because they are apt to demonstrate the process physically, communicate verbally and miss out on important details for posterity. While the former can be an effective way to train, what it is not, is a holistic approach that should include documentation for the trainee to follow once the expert is no longer available. This will be an exercise in developing your Operational Definitions; establishing a uniform way the business will operate. On the following page are some tips on writing your documentation.

1) Avoid over-estimating the performers' knowledge.

While I mentioned this before, I reiterate it here and place it first on the list to stress its importance. Assuming competence in a given skill set, even one that was vetted during the interview process, can lead to costly employee mistakes. Take the time to write detailed instructions as if for someone with no knowledge of the process and could simply "walk in off the street" and begin working if he or she follows the steps. Even if the person has the skill set, they will still need to know how it is done within the particular organization, a way which could be significantly different from what they are accustomed to within other organizations.

2) Assume Performer Competency.

While this may seem contradictory to the previous tip, it is actually countering for the opposite extreme. Employees should have a certain basic skill set in order to have been hired in the first place. An example of a process step that has too much detail would be the following:

a) Turn the dial marked Temperature on the pizza oven in a counter clockwise fashion from 0 to the 450° Fahrenheit marking and wait till the orange light comes on, indicating that the oven has reached its desired temperature.

The previous contains excess detail and unnecessary information. An employee should have basic knowledge on how to turn the oven's temperature dial. A better way to say this is:

a) Set the Temperature of the Pizza Oven to 450° Fahrenheit.

3) Scope

Lengthy instructions that try to include multiple processes all at once should be avoided. If you find that your instructions are growing beyond a couple pages, consider segregating them into logical Start and Stop pieces. For instance, writing a process that includes unloading the flour from the delivery truck, storing it, then mixing it to create the dough, then tossing the dough in preparation for spreading the sauce, is an excellent example of Scope Creep. Document processes separately, where possible.

Also, it is ideal to document your processes such that they line up one after another. If you could place the work instructions of all of your processes one on top of another, then someone should be able to, in theory, start at the top of the stack and got through all of the processes of your business from top to bottom, where the stop and start of each process would be a separate stapled packet. This is a strong indicator of a well-documented business. As an example, if the final step of one process is to store a loaf of dough in the fridge, then have the next set of instructions begin with taking the loaf of dough out of the fridge before rolling it out. Adhering to this method greatly increases the flow of documentation and eases the location of the same.

4) Leverage Intellectual Capital

Standardization of verbiage throughout your documentation is key to ensuring that the team is speaking a common language. Using different vocabulary is the Mother of all miscommunications. If you refer to the pizza sauce as just 'sauce' in one document and 'red sauce' in another, this will cause ambiguity. Imagine the pizza baker asking an assistant to bring him some more 'sauce' according to the instructions and he comes back with 'red sauce' which turns out to be marinara sauce instead of pizza sauce. This results in waste in the form of time loss and increases the potential for an incorrect ingredient being placed in the customer's order. Likewise, if there are common steps that occur across multiple processes, do not hesitate to use that exact verbiage. It will save time in writing the documents and creates familiarity when performers encounter the verbiage across multiple processes. It will also make it easier to update your processes if that common verbiage thread should change. You would just need to switch it out with Find & Replace.

5) Best Case Scenario

Hopefully, your process does not have a lot of anomalies that have to be tediously explained. If so, then it will be one ripe with opportunities for improvement and you will want to prioritize for application of the tools in this book. That being said, your process should be written as if it were running smoothly with minimal caveats that have to be explained away. What would you consider to be the "Happy Path," the path which would be ideal for the flow of the process? For example, if your oven has a faulty temperature gauge and you have a step that has a comment in parentheses like the following, then I recommend leaving the "fix" out of the document. This is something you can place in a risk assessment tool discussed later that will assist in identifying how much of a priority it is to get fixed. In the meantime, document the process as if it were functioning normally.

Example of a Process Step requiring needless over-explaining:

Step 7: Ensure that the temperature light is on and then place the pizza into the oven. (if the oven temperature light is flickering then give it three whacks and it should stay on)

Also, avoid providing needless background as to why a step has to be performed a certain way. This is not the moment to give a history lesson. Stick with what the performer really needs to know. They can learn about the history of it through experience. An example of verbiage in a process step that you should avoid is as follows:

Step 7: Ensure that the temperature light is on and then place the pizza into the oven. (The reason you have to make sure it's on is because it doesn't always work because there is faulty wiring from when a technician was here trying to fix something else and accidentally cut the wrong wire and didn't tape it right.)

6) Performers Usually Know Best

Employees are your greatest asset. If they are already performing the process then they will most likely know how to do it better than you do and have already worked out the "path of least resistance." You will be wise to work in conjunction with them to create the instructions to ensure effective documentation. It is also advisable to indicate who performs the process. Clearly defined roles avoid confusion and potential conflicts within the team. It is also prudent to identify roles that are cross-trained on the process that can serve as a backup in the likelihood that the primary performer is unavailable due to other priorities or absence. Avoid; however, documenting specific names of employees in the documentation. Their title or role should suffice. A separate document can be kept that identifies which employees have which titles or roles. It also eases the necessity to update documentation anytime you may have turnover.

7) The Auditor Lens

This is applicable more so for those industries where an outside organization, or Internal Compliance, conducts audits for adherence to regulations: however, it is just as important for smaller entities. While writing your instructions, looking at your process for risks and gaps through the scrutinizing eyes of an auditor will serve you well when it comes time for an actual audit. If you were the auditor, what would you be looking to catch?

8) Testing

Ideally, you will test process with a performer that has not been involved with the documentation, thus far. Having a fresh set of eyes walk through the instructions while performing the process will provide great insight to see if it is complete and easy to follow by someone that has little to no previous knowledge. Capture any opportunities where this performer is asking for clarification, giving suggestions, or otherwise providing feedback and update your instructions accordingly.

9) Accessibility

Once you have written, tested and are comfortable with your instructions, ensure that they are accessible to the performer. Locking them up in a file cabinet or on a hard drive defeats the purpose. If there are changes in the process, it is imperative that the documentation is updated and that the change is communicated to the team. Failure to do so results in disconnects with what is the proper procedure and a loss of confidence in the documentation. Provide a date that the document was created and when the next update should occur. This will establish a clear expectation and ensure accountability among those that are responsible for maintaining the documentation. It goes without saying; however, that appropriate back-up and storage measures should always be exercised to ensure business continuity.

10) Quality Control

Not to contradict my recommendation of writing your process "as is" and worry about improvement later, if you do have steps that already exist that are checking for quality, don't forget to include this ever important piece. If you are identifying opportunities for process improvement, be sure to capture them so that you can review them once you are ready to take steps to improve your process. We will build on this in the Improve chapter.

The aforementioned ten tips are general guidelines for writing instructions and, if adhered to, should result in having a thorough and well-defined understanding of your business. This documentation will provide the needed skeletal structure for your enterprise as you begin to pack on the muscle of success.

Written instruction is not the only effective way to document your processes. We, as humans, are visual creatures and absorb information faster when it is presented to us in an format that is easier for us to internalize. Process Maps are extremely effective in achieving this and I am an avid proponent of their use. Shortly after writing your instructions, I highly recommend using them to create Process Maps. It is but another medium to document the process, but it can be much more than that. It can be an opportunity to identify gaps, risks, rework and needed controls. Powerful software such as Microsoft Visio is ideal for creating them; however, other programs within the Office suite can be just as effective, albeit a bit more tedious. There are other mapping software products on the market so take some time to research what works best for you. Technology is here to help us, not hinder us, so invest some effort now to identify those tools that can best assist you with achieving your objectives. If you are not tech savvy, this will be one area where it is important to learn this important skill. The success of your business depends on it.

On the next page is an example of a Process Map for the preparation of a Large Cheese Pizza. Note that there are clear Start and End bubbles and that the process steps are simple and clearly separated from each other. Not to oversimplify the Process Map, but it is powerful in delivering to the performer clear expectations and clarity around the order in which the steps are to be performed.

Also note, the decision diamond. These are useful for indicating any variable paths within the process and allow for compensation of potential frequent anomalies. Also, attempt to find an appropriate cruising altitude as you "fly over" or document your process, otherwise it will be disjointed. For example, if you have a process step that says, "Place the chopped green peppers on the pizza no more than one inch from each other" and the next step is "Place red peppers on the pizza," then you have a disconnect on your level of granularity and should adjust for consistency. Remember that your Process Flow should follow, allowing for revisions on both sides, your long form written instructions and, again, be sure to adhere to the 'Happy Path' philosophy.

Fig. F

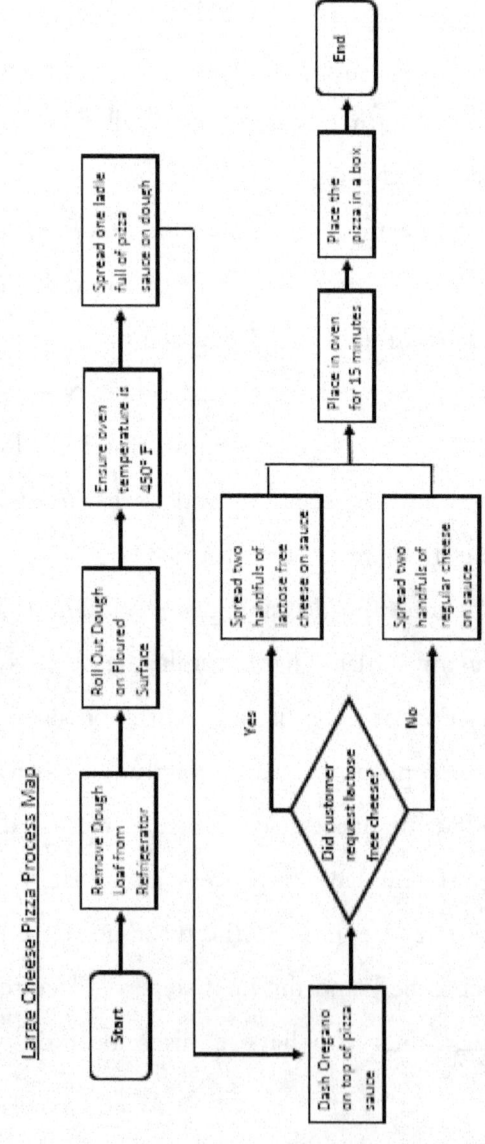

Large Cheese Pizza Process Map

People have different ways of learning and computing information. While written instructions may be sufficient for some, a visual of the process in the form of a Process Flow Map, as shown in *Fig. F* on the opposing page, is highly effective for those of us who can better capture the overall process through this more visual medium. There are advantages to processing symbols and pictographs over tedious and lengthy written instruction.

One other alternate way to document your process is what is called a SIPOC, an acronym for Suppliers, Inputs, Process, Output, and Customers. Where a Process Map may fly over at about 20, 000 feet, the SIPOC will be higher level, say around 35,000 feet. It is important to understand that a Supplier is not what you might think of in the traditional sense of a vendor that supplies raw material to your business, but rather all instances where something, the Input, is being supplied to the step within the process. Inversely, the Customer is not exclusively the one who walks in up to the counter of the proverbial storefront, but any and all recipients of the Output of the Process Step.

In *Fig. G*, on the following page, I start by identifying 4-6 high level steps and place them in the middle column with the header of "Process." I then identify what Input(s) are needed to complete this step and the Output(s) that are produced.

Finally, I identify who Supplies those Inputs and who are the Customers of the Outputs. Note that: it is typical for the Customer of the previous process step to be the Supplier of the next step forming a backwards "S" shape, if you will, as we progress through. This is effective to ensure continuity with handoffs within the process. A SIPOC will provide you a unique perspective, as it assists in identifying the resources of suppliers, customers, inputs, and outputs needed to perform the process. While not one of the more crucial tools of Process Improvement, it is good exercise to perform because the more angles that you view your process from, the greater understanding you will have of it and the more opportunities you will identify.

Fig. G

SIPOC for Pizza Preperation Process

Supplier	Input	Process	Output	Customer
Pantry	Flour, Salt, Water	Make Dough	Raw Dough	Refrigerator
Pantry, Refrigerator	Tomatoes, Basil, Garlic	Make Sauce	Prepared Sauce	Refrigerator
Refrigerator	Dough, Sauce	Make Pizza	Prepared Pizza	Oven
Oven	Heat, Timer	Bake Pizza	Baked Pizza	End Customer

Lastly, a tool called a Responsibility Matrix or RACI (Responsible, Accountable, Consult, and Inform) can display who should be doing what within the process and their relationships with each other, if any. *Fig H* is a completed matrix for the "Large Pepperoni Pizza Assembly Process."

Fig. H

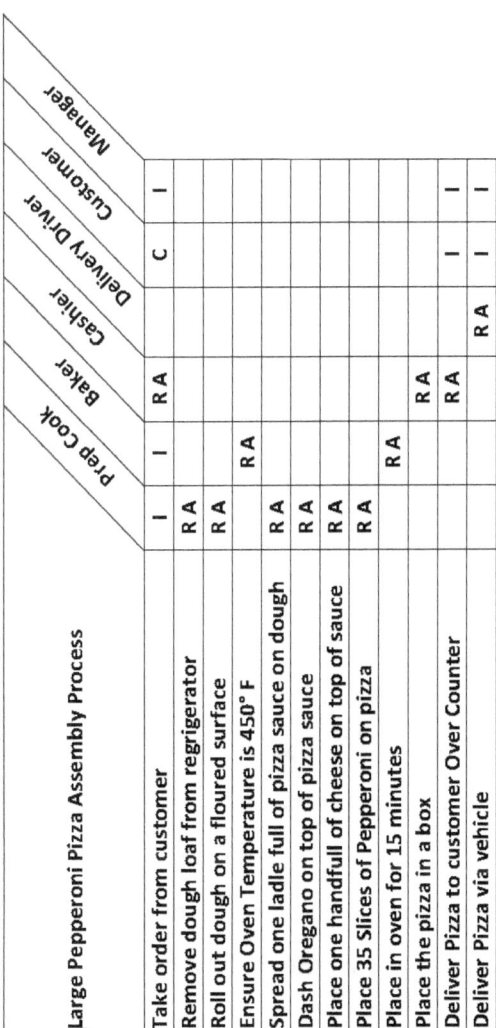

Large Pepperoni Pizza Assembly Process	Prep Cook	Baker	Cashier	Delivery Driver	Customer	Manager
Take order from customer	I		R A		C	I
Remove dough loaf from regrigerator	R A					
Roll out dough on a floured surface	R A					
Ensure Oven Temperature is 450° F		R A				
Spread one ladle full of pizza sauce on dough	R A					
Dash Oregano on top of pizza sauce	R A					
Place one handfull of cheese on top of sauce	R A					
Place 35 Slices of Pepperoni on pizza	R A					
Place in oven for 15 minutes		R A				
Place the pizza in a box		R A				
Deliver Pizza to customer Over Counter			R A		I	I
Deliver Pizza via vehicle				R A	I	I

Below are descriptions of each type of designations.

Responsible - person who actually performs that task, there will always be an "R" designation for each step because someone must be responsible for actually performing the process step. It is possible to have multiple types of performers designated as "R" and it is likely that the person that is responsible is also Accountable.

Accountable - person who holds decision authority for the process step, there will always be an "A" designation for each step because someone has to be accountable for making decisions, however there should never be more than one "A" per step as this could result in waste with conflicting individuals with approval authority. It is possible to have an "R A" designation for a performer in any given process step as they may be both responsible and accountable.

Consult - persons within the process that should be consulted before actioning the step. Typically this is someone that has information or material that is needed in order to proceed. It is not necessary to combine Consult with any other designation as it is understood that if someone is Responsible or Accountable that they will be consulted as well.

Inform - a person that needs to be notified that the step is taking place. These are usually managers or perhaps someone that performs quality assurance on the process. It is not necessary to combine Inform with any other designation as it is understood that if someone is Responsible or Accountable that they will be informed as well.

So, for the step of "Take order from customer," the cashier is both Responsible and Accountable for this step. He or she will Consult with the customer to take their order and Inform the Prep Cook and Baker so that they can be ready for their roles in the process. The manager is also informed be it real-time; "Hey! We've got an order!" or through reporting of how many orders were taken that day. A Responsibility Matrix is an ideal way to avoid confusion among performers and ensure that roles are defined.

In conclusion, there are many ways to document a process. While it may seem tedious at first to do this you will find great value in performing this all important step in process improvement as it provides a baseline for you to begin your story. Without it, you will have not have a tangible starting point to begin your journey, so invest some time up front for this and prepare to reap the rewards later.

IVAN G. BANNOWSKY

4

Measure and Analyze

"Measure Twice, Cut Once"

- English Proverb

After having clearly defined and documented your processes, it's time to get into the heart of process improvement. To accomplish this, you will first need to figure out what it is that needs to be improved through the collection of data. Anecdotal observations will not be enough to determine which areas you should target. Real tangible measurements will allow you to build a solid case. While there are many ways to improve a process, typically, "Speed of Execution" of the process, is the area of greatest opportunity for wins. So with that premise, we'll begin there.

In our Pizza Shop example, we will use hypothetical data on how long it takes to make a Large Pepperoni Pizza under ideal circumstances. In other words, the steps within the process would have minimal or no anomalies nor opportunities for rework. Rework being a step or steps that would need to be repeated in order to ensure quality. An example of rework would be if, during the building of the pizza, the prep cook accidentally put sausage on the pizza instead of pepperoni and the baker realizes it just before putting it in the oven. He then sends it back to the prep cook to remove the sausages and replace them with pepperoni.

The collection of data can be a delicate subject for your team, as they will surely interpret this as an assessment of their performance, especially if it is outside any current ongoing public indicators. It is important that you meet with the team so that they understand that you are collecting data solely on the process itself and not individual performers. As you will be collecting data on multiple performers, it is advisable not to share the results of the performers' time that it takes for them to complete the process. If you do share the results, I recommend that you mask the names of your employees with surnames such as Performer 1 and Performer 2 to ensure there are no bruised egos. Competition can be healthy, but this is not the time for it. Stress the fact that this is not a race and that they should move through the process as they normally would so that you can capture the most accurate data possible. Also, if possible, do not capture the duration of how long it takes one performer to complete the process while they are doing so in front of another performer. This will surely make them self-conscious and nervous. Not only would this be unfair and potentially create unnecessary animosity, it could also produce data that may not be reflective of how the process is performed under normal circumstances because the performer may attempt to do it faster than normal to "show off," if you will.

Create a spreadsheet that has all the steps of the process listed in one column and then an additional column next to it where you will capture the time it takes to complete the corresponding step. It is preferable to capture two data sets from each performer to ensure consistency and that there is sufficient volume of data on which to base an analysis and hypothesis. If possible, perform the data captures on different days. Attempting to do one after another may not simulate the real day-to-day routine especially if it is a process that is not repeated one after another for extended durations.

On the following page is a Data Collection Tool that a business owner or manager could use to action the Large Pepperoni Pizza process. *Fig. I* consists of a blank template to review without the clutter of data. The Data Collection Tool is populated with data generated for illustrative purposes only. Note that the average of the two performers and the two data sets comes to 131.75 seconds, about 2 minutes and 12 seconds, to make a Large Pepperoni Pizza for the process as it is documented. This does not include the 15 minutes it takes to bake the pizza. This was purposely left out as this is a finite mechanical measurement that does not require human intervention and therefore would not sway the final count of the total process time one way or another. Only those metrics that had a possibility of a variation should be measured and these are typically those that are performed by humans. There are some mechanical steps that could have variation; however. If this is the case, that could be an indicator of a faulty mechanism which would require investigation.

Fig. I

Large Pepperoni Pizza Assembly Process	Performer 1		Performer 2		Average
	Data Set 1	Data Set 2	Data Set 1	Data Set 2	
Remove dough loaf from regrigerator					
Roll out dough on a floured surface					
Ensure Oven Temperature is 450° F					
Spread one ladle full of pizza sauce on dough					
Dash Oregano on top of pizza sauce					
Place one handfull of cheese on top of sauce					
Place 35 Slices of Pepperoni on pizza					
Place in oven for 15 minutes					
Place the pizza in a box					
Total in Seconds					

Large Pepperoni Pizza Assembly Process	Performer 1		Performer 2		Average
	Data Set 1	Data Set 2	Data Set 1	Data Set 2	
Remove dough loaf from regrigerator	16	15	17	15	15.75
Roll out dough on a floured surface	25	23	22	24	23.5
Ensure Oven Temperature is 450° F	7	8	4	5	6
Spread one ladle full of pizza sauce on dough	8	9	8	10	8.75
Dash Oregano on top of pizza sauce	5	5	6	5	5.25
Place one handfull of cheese on top of sauce	9	12	9	11	10.25
Place 35 Slices of Pepperoni on pizza	37	42	39	41	39.75
Place in oven for 15 minutes	11	13	10	8	10.5
Place the pizza in a box	13	14	11	10	12
Total in Seconds	131	141	126	129	131.75

Also, note that the two performers completed each step of the process relatively close to each other on each data set capture. Again, you will need to judge if the variations are within expectable ranges. If they are not, then some investigation as to why there are broader than normal fluctuations should be conducted. Were there other anomalies not unaccounted for, perhaps? Was one performer distracted by other activities during the collection of the data or have a completely different way of performing the step? It is important that the performers are equally focused on performing the task and that they are doing so in a relatively similar fashion.

In the data you've collected, look for the step that requires the most time to complete. This is where there will most likely be the greatest opportunity for improvement. This is not to say that other steps in the process could not be made more efficient but the justification here being that; where there is the most mass, in terms of cycle time, than potentially the more waste exists that can be reduced relatively. The step of "Place 35 Slices of Pepperoni on pizza" resulted in the highest cycle time to complete at an average of about 40 seconds. It is more likely that you will be able to reduce this by a few seconds or more as opposed to attempting to reduce the time of "Ensure Oven Temperature is 450° F" which only took an average of 6 seconds to perform. It is less probable to shave a second or more off this process step as there is less "mass" from which to do so. Therefore, the step requiring 40 seconds to complete should be your first area of focus. We will revisit this in the "Improve" chapter.

Here is another example where collecting data and analyzing it can assist in identifying if we are meeting the customer's expectations as discussed in the Survey Map. In this example, we will measure the time that it takes for a customer to receive the pizza delivered to their door from the time that the pizza leaves the shop. We'll assume that the shop has a delivery radius that is achievable to deliver within 35 minutes; the timeframe that most customers expressed was their preference in the survey. We will also assume that there are no other anomalies such as construction, traffic, or weather, which would be factors out of our control anyway. We'll also say that the number of deliveries, drivers and the time of day, say around lunchtime, are constant. In *Fig. J*, on the following page, is an example of what that data might look like if delivery times and a tally of those times were collected on a given day. The "Time Out" stamp indicates when the driver left the pizza shop and the "Delivered" Time Stamp is when they reached the customer's door.

Fig. J

Pizza Delivery

Time Out	Delivered	Duration*
11:10am	11:25am	15
11:13am	11:32am	18
11:17am	11:37am	20
11:18am	11:40am	22
11:20am	11:44am	24
11:25am	11:49am	24
11:25am	11:51am	26
11:27am	11:52am	26
11:29am	11:55am	26
11:30am	11:56am	26
11:31am	12:05pm	34
11:35am	12:09pm	34
11:39am	12:13pm	34
11:41am	12:15pm	34
11:42am	12:16pm	34
11:44am	12:18pm	34
11:47am	12:23pm	36
11:50am	12:26pm	36
11:57am	12:33pm	36
12:02pm	12:38pm	36
12:04pm	12:40pm	36
12:08pm	12:46pm	38
12:09pm	12:47pm	38
12:10pm	12:48pm	38
12:14pm	12:52pm	38
12:19pm	12:57pm	38
12:22pm	1:02pm	40
12:23pm	1:03pm	40
12:25pm	1:13pm	48
12:30pm	1:20pm	50

* in minutes

Pizza Deliery Tally

Seconds	Count
15	1
18	1
20	1
22	1
24	2
26	4
34	6
36	5
38	5
40	2
40	1
48	1
50	1

Fig. K

In *Fig. J*, we have collected the volume of deliveries and their duration as well as tallied the delivery times and their number of occurrences. We have taken the tallies and placed them into a graph in *Fig. K*. Note that the majority of deliveries land in the middle of the graph around the 26 to 38 minute mark. Remember that our goal is to deliver under 35 minutes per our customer's preference. The bell curve on *Fig. K* indicates that the process is functioning as intended with outliers being indicated at the lower ends of the curve and the higher frequency of occurrences being at the peak of the curve. As these land around the 35 minute mark this would be considered its centralized tendency.

This is a great tool to use to measure for targeted performance. If you do not see a bell shaped curve and see a slope or a bell shape curve that has the height of the curve elsewhere other than around your target, then you will need to dig further to understand why this is. It is possible that you will need to adjust your target because you are either underperforming or over-performing, depending on the location of the heights of the curve relative to your goal.

If you are consistently exceeding expectations, resist the urge to pat yourself on the back just yet. While it is great to celebrate successes and boost morale because it looks like you are hitting the mark most of the time, we should also always be striving to do better. Teams become desensitized when they are not challenged. This is not to say, of course, that a process can be infinitely better. There is such a thing as optimal performance levels; however, it is also a good idea to rally the team around achieving greater heights even if that means setting the bar higher, at least temporarily. Be prepared to hear possible moaning, but this is essential to engaging employees, not a means to demoralize them. Keep a close eye on your goals. Prolonged, unrealistic and unobtainable goals can cause the team's morale to plummet. This could be perceived as a deliberate attempt to block achievement, especially where there is performance accountability and financial incentive, and it could be a long road to bring that morale back up to acceptable levels. An example of a bell shape curve on either end of your data are as follows.

Fig. L

Fig. M

A slope in our data, either falling off towards the higher delivery times, as in *Fig. L,* or steeping up, as in *Fig. M*, due to higher and higher delivery times, indicates that our expectation for delivering within 35 minutes is not realistic and that we may need to reassess our delivery commitment. We may need to find a tradeoff. For example, we may need to change our motto to "We Deliver High Quality Pizzas Anywhere within City Limits in 40 Minutes or Less." Note that we inform the customer that there is a tradeoff. It may take us longer but it's a higher quality pizza and we cover a greater area. Granted, the sloping could also be due to some other systemic underlying issue. Steeping up could also mean that we do not have enough drivers and are not meeting demand. Falling off could indicate that the food is ready too fast and perhaps undercooked resulting in poor quality. It could also mean that we don't have enough business to sustain the number of drivers we have on staff or that we need to conduct a marketing campaign to bring in new business and generate more deliveries.

Another important analysis to conduct would be of those anomalies within your process that would be considered either Common Cause or Special Cause. Common Cause indicates that there is a miss of our goal that occurs commonly, perhaps a failure to meet customer expectations on Mondays because there is only one Pizza Baker on this day when on all others there are two. Special Cause can occur, where perhaps the one oven stopped working on one day out of the entire year resulting in a spike in delivery times.

Customers typically do not like variation of delivery. The tighter the data points are to the mean, then the more efficient the process is and the happier your customer will be. The less variance in your process then the more predictable it is and the more customers will come to rely on the product or service. Increased precision around your target is the goal.

It is also important to identify what potentially could go wrong with your process, which is identified as Risk, in addition to what triggers should be in place to indicate that something is not functioning optimally or that it is producing defects. Having these controls and contingency plans in place will lend assurances to essential and critical processes within your organization as well as avoidances of stoppages or worse. As business owners and managers, we don't like to think of catastrophe; however, the adage of "an ounce of prevention is worth a pound of cure" is quite relevant here. This will require you to look at your process and play the role of the pessimist, envisioning scenarios that one hopes will never happen but for which we should be prepared. Engage employees for this exercise, they will have unique insight into what has been and what potentially can go wrong.

In our Pizza Shop example, let's again take a look at the Large Pepperoni Pizza process and identify our areas of risk. This can best be captured by creating a Failure-Cause-Control

Analysis similar to the one represented by *Fig. N.* For this exercise, I'm going to leverage some of the process steps from my Process Flow Map that I would have created for the Large Pepperoni Pizza process, which is similar to the Large Cheese Pizza process cited in Chapter 3 - Documentation.

Fig. N

Large Pepperoni Pizza Assembly Process	Potential Failure	Cause	Control	Priority
Remove dough loaf from refrigerator	Dough not at right temperature	Fridge at wrong temperature	Daily Fridge checks	Medium
Roll out dough on a floured surface	Dough not rolled to write size and thickness	Prep Cook inattentive or inexperienced	Quality checks by Pizza Baker	Low
Ensure Oven Temperature is 450° F	Temperature is too high or too low	Broken oven	Weekly independent thermometer check	High
Place in oven for 15 minutes	Baked for too long or too little	Confusion with which pizza is being timed	Multiple Timers for multiple pizzas	High

For each process step, you'll want to identify one or more potential failures. The election of these potential failures will depend on how great the propensity is for those failures to occur. For the step of "Remove dough loaf from refrigerator," I have identified that a Potential Failure could be that the dough is not at the right temperature and that the Cause could be that the refrigerator was not at the right temperature at the time As for a Control, I have identified checking the fridge temperature on a daily basis to ensure it is where it should be. On a prioritization scale I have identified this as a "Medium" due to the level of severity and potentiality for occurrence.

Certainly, there are many other things that could go wrong with the step of removing the dough from the refrigerator. Perhaps, I might grab the Large size dough that was intended for a Medium pizza or maybe I grab a raw dough loaf that contains gluten for an order requesting gluten-free dough. Both of these would result in a less than desirable experience for the customer and therefore should be considered a risk. You will want to identify as many possible potential failures as well as the causes of those failures to ensure you have proper controls in place in the event of their occurrences. Remember that Risk is anything that could expose an employee to harm, the company to a regulatory infraction or sanction, loss of revenue or loss of customer-base as well as general inefficiency within the process.

Another important method that can be used to analyze your process is a Root Cause Analysis. An effective tool to accomplish this is called the 5 Why Exercise. It is equivalent to the small inquisitive child that asks "Why is the sky blue?" or other similar questions and then proceeds to question the answer with another "Why?" If there is a breakdown in the process or there are outliers occurring at either end of the bell curve of your data, applying the 5 Why Exercise can assist in identifying the root cause of the issue at hand.

There is no law that says that you must exhaust all of the 5 Whys. The intent, rather, is to dig deep enough to identify the root cause as well as the solution that prevents that cause or at least enact a Control to alarm in the event of its occurrence. On the following page, *Fig. O* is an example of what the 5 Why Tool could look like if the pizza dough is not at the right temperature when removed from the refrigerator as part of the Large Pepperoni pizza process where we identified risk in *Fig. F*. In this example, note that we are able to find a sufficient solution within 4 Whys, so as you can see, it is not imperative to do five, rather enough to achieve the desired outcome of identifying the root cause.

Fig. O

Root Cause Analysis

Potential Failure	Why?	Why?	Why?	Why?	Solution
Pizza Dough not at right temperature	Refrigerator thermostat had been changed	Prep Cook thought temperature was supposed to be lower	Prep Cook not properly trained and correct temperature is not posted by thermostat	Training is inadequate and no one has ever thought to post the correct temperature next to thermostat	Incorporate into written training the correct temperature for refrigerator and make a sign to post next to the thermostat.

So, where the Potential Failure lies in that the pizza dough it not at the right temperature, I would ask my first why and the answer would be that the refrigerator thermostat had been changed. So then I'll again ask, "Well why was that?" and the response being that the prep cook thought that the temperature was supposed to be lower. I would continue this until I could find the root cause and identify a solution to minimize its recurrence. In this case it would be to revise training and post a sign next to the thermostat that states what the temperature setting should be of the refrigerator. While this may seem like an obvious solution, it is surprising how effective this tool can be because it walks you through putting the issue down on paper instead of trying to figure it all out in an imaginary space. It may not be obvious to the performer until it is put before them. There is much to be said about slowing the process down to an "instant slow-mo replay" to take a good look at what is occurring at the scene of the crime, if you will, and identify opportunities.

The last concept within analyzing your process that I would like to touch on is that of identifying what adds value to it and what kind of value should be included. There are essentially three kinds of Value; Customer Value Add, Business Value Add, and Non-Value Add. Customer Value Add or CVA is identified as those steps within the process that the customer is willing to pay for in order to get the desired product or service. For example, in the step of spreading one ladle of pizza on the dough, this is something the customer is willing to pay for because they want pizza sauce on their pizza.

Business Value Add is a step that really only benefits the business. As an example, if you have a step where you are tallying the number of pizzas that you make as part of the actual process of preparing the pizza; then that is something that only benefits the business to know. The customer is not concerned with whether you know how many pizzas you make and the man-hours that it takes to record this; therefore it is not something the customer would be willing to pay for.

Lastly, there is Non-Value Add, which implies a step that adds no value to the process whatsoever. For example, if there is a step to include a sheet of wax paper on the bottom of the pizza box to avoid grease leakage and the box has a coating of wax on it already anyway, then this would be something that would add no value to the process. This serves neither the customer nor the business and is most likely waste in all senses of the word. Typically, these non-value add steps are either antiquated or were never updated to reflect changes to the process. Case in point; the new wax coated pizza boxes that were ordered should have negated the step to place a wax sheet on the bottom. Proper procedure dictates that this would have been updated in the training and documentation. Since is was not, it resulted in wasted expenses of person-hours and material.

These are just a few of the more commonly used methods by which to measure and analyze your process and you will no doubt find other ways to do so with the specialized processes within your organization. The important thing is to ensure that you have a firm understanding of how your process can be measurable and identify pressure points of failure. This will allow you to identify and implement areas requiring process improvement efforts, which we will cover in the next chapter. Likewise you will identify and implement Controls and quality assurance precautions, which we will cover in the subsequent chapter.

IVAN G. BANNOWSKY

5

Improve

"Without continual growth and progress, such words as improvement, achievement, and success have no meaning."

- Benjamin Franklin

Now that you've measured and analyzed your processes it's time to find ways to improve them. A great way to do this is to find areas where there is waste. Waste is essentially anything that adds expense or time to the process without actually adding value. Waste typically comes in the forms of Movement, Mistakes, Stock, Over-production, Extra-Processing, and Under-utilized Talent. Let's take a look at each of these a little more in depth.

1) Movement

There are many forms of movement and just as many forms of waste therein. Essentially, it is the time it takes to move something within the process. For example, it could be the transport of inventory from one location to another, be it by vehicle or by hand. If I have a chain of pizza shops, it's going to be a good idea for me to find the best way to have inventory moved around amongst them, in effort to be logistically efficient.

This could also apply within the kitchen. If I have to transport the pizza dough from the refrigerator to the far side of the kitchen to prepare, then walk all the way back across the kitchen to the oven, there is a lot of waste here, illustrated in this Inefficient Kitchen Layout in *Fig. P*.

Fig. P

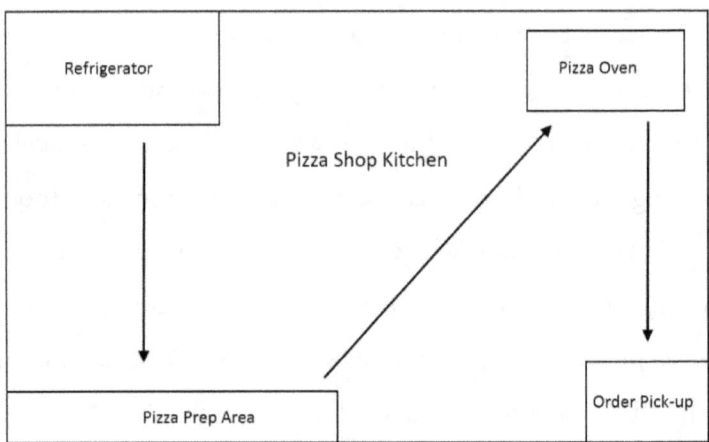

Fig. Q

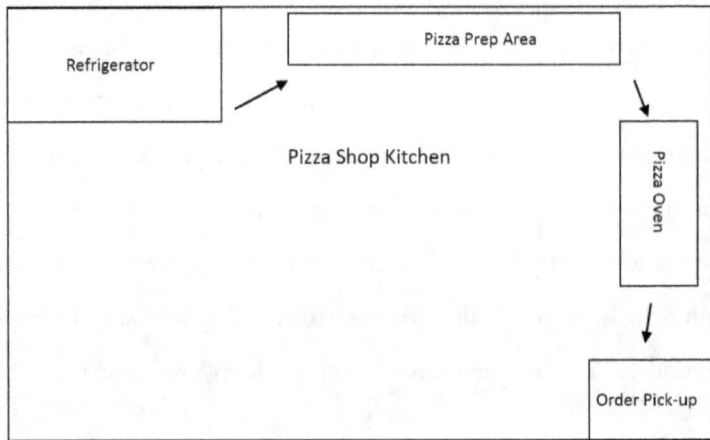

Moving stations around would result in a much more Efficient Kitchen Layout, *Fig. Q.* Ergonomics is the study of efficiency in their working environment like working in front of a computer with ergonomic keyboards, mice and chairs. This is also relatable to software interface design. If you have a process that requires a button be pressed after filling in a field, it makes sense to place that button close to that field instead of placing it way on the other side of the interface. It takes time for the arrow to travel from the field to the button. While this may seem like a small facet in scale, imagine the aggregate of the thousands of times that action is performed multiplied by the number of performers. Seconds add up to minutes, minutes to hours, and time is money. Movement Waste can occur, not just in the transport of materials and product, but in delivering information, as well.

2) Standby

Instances where process cannot move forward, known as bottlenecks or waiting should be targeted for elimination due to their prominent role among inefficiencies. An example could be if a prep cook has to wait for another prep cook to finish with the pizza preparation table. If the demand, the available space, and the cost-to-benefit ratio warrant it, an additional prep table should be installed to allow the simultaneous preparation of multiple orders.

3) Skill

I'll reiterate here that your greatest assets are your people and their skill sets. I have often seen great talent not being leveraged where it was needed and from which could have easily been tapped. Provide opportunities for employees to exhibit their talents and you will see some of your future leaders emerge and shine. This should also include cross-training of performers to ensure backups. You will surely be surprised of what your employees are capable. They just need a chance. You are where you are today because someone took a chance on you, so don't forget to pass the baton. Also, any time you have process performers actioning waste, there is a double whammy, because of the people resources being dedicated to that waste, in addition to the waste itself.

4) Over-processing

This is where unnecessary steps in the process do not add value to the end output. For example, if the prep cook washes the green pepper, dices it, then washes the cut up green pepper again, this would not be needed as it was already sufficiently washed the first time around. The customer will be sufficiently satisfied with the preliminary wash and will not be willing to pay for the additional and unnecessary wash.

5) Mistakes

A process that is error-prone will be costly and result in waste as it is known in the traditional sense in terms of inventory that must be thrown away or the time needed to redo the task.

6) Overproduction/Inventory

The production of excess product within the process that may cause bottlenecks. This would include the storage and the cost to maintain end product that is not moving out fast enough.

7) Waiting

Any resource, be it hardware or people, standing idly by waiting to action their step of the process or where their usage is not optimized is considered waiting for the next step.

All these forms of waste can be reviewed, and hopefully eliminated, through a series of tools including the Kaizen, which is a working session that brings in all performers, process managers, experts, and management to improve the process. We will discuss this further later in this chapter.

The inverse of these forms of waste are efficiency techniques known as "5S" which are outlined as follows.

Sort - Ensure that only items that are needed are present in the process step. Remove those that do not belong to avoid clutter and disarray.

Streamline - Place process steps in order, as well as those items needed to perform each step, in an easily accessible and prioritized manner.

Shine - Maintain the workspace clean and free from distractions or "dirt" that may cause hardware to deteriorate or get in the way of performing the process efficiently.

Standardize - Ensure consistency across workstations and processes to minimize ambiguity.

Sustain - Monitor for adherence to all of the above, performing audits and reviews of documentation.

Defect prevention is another effective way to improve your process. This can be accomplished by identifying what, within your process, is prone to mistakes or errors as well as methods to prevent them. Think of it as almost like child-proofing your home with electrical outlet covers and cabinet locks. As an example, if your pizza oven never needs to exceed a temperature of 450° F, then either place a sign by the temperature dial to never turn pass that temperature or better yet, find a way to mechanically prevent the dial from being turned any higher.

Lastly, the following three tools that I'll discuss are Work In Progress (WIP), Exit Rate, and Little's Law. These are considered a bit more advanced in the realm of Process Improvement; however, I think they are worth mentioning here for those that are interested in next level tools.

"Work in Progress" refers to the number of pieces that are currently going through the process. Often it is just one piece, depending on the scope of the start and finish of the process. However, it is conceivable that multiple pieces may be going through the process at varying stages of assembly. When this is the case, Little's Law applies which states that the Exit Rate or capacity of the process cannot exceed the number of widgets that can be worked on at a time. In other words, I can't assemble 3 pizzas at a time when I have only one prep cook with two hands. While not an Earth-shattering revelation, it is important that there is awareness around this concept to understand that; simply by pulling levers and adjusting variables within the process will not make it produce more and more widgets infinitely.

All of the aforementioned in this chapter will best be

reviewed in an event called a "Kaizen." It is an opportunity for the team to meet and discuss ideas for improvement. When conducting a Kaizen it is imperative that you inform the team of what specifically it is that is being looked at for improvement and to review the following rules with them.

Kaizen Rules

1) Be Flexible and Positive

2) Focus on Solutions, not the Problem

3) All Opinions are equal, even those from Management

4) Participation is Key

As the facilitator of a Kaizen you will need to foster an atmosphere of openness and engagement from all. Healthy debate is good and trust that logic will prevail. Remember that, where true collaboration happens, there is compromise. This will be a session to actually take action, not one where there is only the development of a plan to take action.

Go through the written process steps one-by-one and review process flows, if they exist. Focus only on one process at a time. Attempts to look at multiple processes will result in a scope creep trap and will surely muddle the team's focus. Perform the process together, in slow-motion, if need be. Don't be afraid to get your hands dirty and some flour on your nose. Only then will you be able to appreciate the process and the team will appreciate your vested interest. As a leader, you can't manage from behind a closed office door. Ask the team to look for forms of waste that can be eliminated and opportunities to apply the 5S Tool. Processes are hardly ever running at their best possible cycle time. There is always room for improvement, lest you achieve the 'Perfect Process.'

Draft new process steps and process flows right there on the spot if changes are made. Build a tangible prototype out of paperclips and index cards, if you need to, capturing any new concepts. Encourage free thinking and removal of any and all constraints when soliciting ideas. Ask, "How could we improve this process if there were no financial or even physical constraints?" Ask the simple and direct question of, "How do we make your job easier?" While you may hear a few ideas that are too lofty, you will be surprised how this will help free up the creative process and how many good ideas can come it. Even if the general idea may be cost or physically prohibitive, there are usually concepts that stem from these that can be applied or a variation done at a lower cost or physicality. At the other extreme, avoid Draconian measures such as eliminating the entire kitchen just because there was a fly in the soup.

Be sure to capture any and all ideas. One effective way to do this is to give all team members sticky notes to write ideas and have them post on a wall. You can then review these as a team to capture those that can reviewed further for implementation, who will own it and a target date for its completion. Prioritize these by which are easiest and the least labor intensive to implement. If necessary, run a pilot of the process before putting into production. Where possible, phase in process steps and test their functionality, before attempting to revamp the entire process which could result in a costly and unnecessary overhaul.

While it is important to focus on processes themselves, don't lose sight of other areas for potential improvements. For example, if you only have one counter person and you have a long line of customers waiting to have their order taken, you are running the risk of customers giving up and going elsewhere or not even approaching, dreading the long wait. Hopefully, you will have these pain points of growth and need to add a second counter person; however, be sure that your processes in the back of the business can handle the demand. It will do neither you nor the customer any good to be able to take orders twice as fast while still only being able to produce a fixed number of pizzas in a fixed amount of time. You may need to hire more bakers, get another oven, and a set up a new prep station to handle the success.

Lastly, keep in mind that simplicity in processes is key. Avoid overcomplicating unnecessarily. Resist caving to complex ideas sent down by higher ups simply to cater to 'better judgement.' Do what makes sense, not what makes someone supposedly look good because they have an idea that no one understands. Ockham's razor is a problem solving principle developed by Philosopher William of Ockham (c. 1287–1347), which states that "Among competing hypotheses, the one with the fewest assumptions should be selected." In other words, the simplest answer is usually the right one.

A few final thoughts as you move to improve your processes. Focus on performers and their interactions, rather than, process steps and tools. Put people first and everything else falls into place. Aim for a functional and efficient process and less about having your documentation perfect. Be flexible and eager to change versus strictly following a plan. There lie your greatest wins.

IVAN G. BANNOWSKY

6

Control

"Quality is not an act. It is a habit."

- Aristotle

Now that you have inspected your process for opportunities to make it more efficient, reduce waste as well as risks, it is time to monitor it for adherence to quality and identify continuous improvement. Process Improvement is never a one-and-done. There is always room for improvement as there is no such thing as "The Perfect Process." A powerful way to monitor the process and engage the team is through Visual Management or VM.

Visual Management is an effective way to keep an eye on how the process is performing, communicate to the team, and capture ideas for improvement. Visual Management can come in many forms; a billboard, whiteboard, or even electronic displays. Regardless of the medium, the intent is the same; to deliver high quality products or services that meet customers' wants and needs while ensuring the success of the business. Process Improvement should always be customer-centric and the more that message is delivered to the team the more they will understand where to focus their energies. VM should house four essential items; Process Flow, Performance, Improvement and Engagement.

Process Flow indicates how the process works and can include the actual display of the flow of the process or at the very least a high-level one. This should also include a brief description of the process and be simple enough to digest with a quick read. An example of a header of a VM Board for the Pizza Prep Process could read like the below.

Pizza Prep Visual Management Board

Purpose: This VM Board displays the process of preparing pizzas and monitors for quality and quantities.

The Performance piece of the VM board should capture metrics of how each performer of the process is performing or the status of each step in the process, depending on what you are attempting to monitor. The goal of each step should be indicated so that all understand the expectation. Metrics known as triggers, which would be just short of the goals, can be indicated so that if the process is in danger of not meeting the expectation, then an alarm, of sorts, will sound and resources can be added to ensure that the goal is met. These metrics should tie back to what is most important to your customers, what you possibly would have captured by surveying them. The purpose of this piece is to indicate how well or not the process is performing. Do not shy away from displaying individual team member's performance. There is nothing wrong with a little healthy competition in this instance. Below, in *Fig. R*, is an example of what a Quality Check part of a Visual Management Board might look like.

Fig. R

Performer	Pizzas Completed	Quality Check
Nino	15	Complete
Luigi	21	Complete
Pepe	13	1 Redo
Mario	10	Complete

Additionally, in *Fig. S* on the following page, a Status Indicator section can show tasks that need to be completed and what the status of that completion is. Color-coding the status is a great way to draw attention to what still needs to be done as opposed to using words, such as "needs attention," which do not carry as much impact. "Green" would indicate that the task is complete or otherwise trending to be completed. "Yellow" being a cautionary state that requires additional attention to ensure that it doesn't go into a red status. Lastly, "Red" would act as an alert that the process step or task requires immediate attention and is at grave risk of not meeting expectation. This simple, yet powerful, tool is the perfect way to communicate at a glance.

Fig. S

Prep for Next Day	Status
Grated Cheese	Green
Diced Peppers	Yellow
Diced Onions	Green
Cut Mushrooms	Red

The third element of Visual Management is Continuous Improvement and should have a dedicated space on the VM Board where the team can voice ideas, concerns, and strategies. They should have an opportunity to gather around the VM board to review the status of performance and provide feedback on a daily basis which is also known as a Daily Stand-up. A matrix indicating who made the suggestion, the idea itself, who will own implantation and the projected completion date should form part of this area.

Free space to post sticky notes should also be made available in this area for those ideas that may come to the team while not in the Daily Stand-up. Encourage the team to always be wearing their Process Improvement Hat. If a brief daily stand-up is not feasible then one should occur as frequently as possible. A stand-up occurring less than once per week will lose its effectiveness. *Fig. T* is one example of what this Process Improvement Matrix could like below.

Fig. T

Date Submitted	Suggestor	Idea	Owner	Status	Target Date
1/20/2016	Mario	Grate cheese beforehand, not during pizza prep	Maria	Green	1/31/2016
1/25/2016	Pepe	Use canned sauce instead of homemade	Maria	Yellow	TBD
1/28/2016	Nino	Deliver pizzas by drone	TBD	Red	TBD

The team will be engaged when they see their ideas displayed for all to see. This is also an opportunity to bring concerns, not just ideas, to the attention of the team. Concerns alone should be welcome and the antiquated thinking of needing to have a solution accompanied with the problem should be demised. The old rule of "Don't bring a problem to the table unless you have a solution" is counterproductive. It sets an expectation that problems should be hidden unless you can figure it out the answer on you own and it places an unnecessary burden on team members. While it is a paradigm shift to do this, allow the team to bring concerns to the forefront individually and to then solve for them collectively as a team. You will soon find that you are creating a community of problem solvers. This should include mistakes that employees have made and that need remediation. It is better to create a culture of rewarding the call out of mistakes so that they can be fixed, rather than one where they are hidden and fester. Mistakes happen in business. The key is how you react to them. Publicly chastising and humiliating employees for their mistakes creates an environment of fear and demoralizes the workforce. It is far better to encourage admission of errors without fear of public shaming which in turn, I have found, will reduce their occurrence.

The fourth and last element of Visual Management is "Team Engagement" which ensures that the team is informed about what is happening and that they have an opportunity to voice ideas. This goes hand in hand with the aforementioned third element of Continuous Improvement in Visual Management. Engagement is called out separately to underline the importance of including the team as part of Process Improvement. Ensure that there is an area on the VM Board for recognition of accomplishments, announcements as well as any other activities that may encourage the team's participation and unity. This should assist in breaking a cycle of complacency. Breaking away from the status quo is a trait that should be encouraged. Do not view this as dissent, rather your own in-house "Think Tank" that you can tap into before needing to seek out a fresh pair of eyes with external consultants. Be sure to allow team members to update the board during the Daily Stand-ups and to capture the date of the last time the team met to reinforce accountability and to indicate how current the board is.

While, yes, it is important to manage, mitigate and otherwise control Risk, beware of over controlling to the point that it strangles the business. There is a certain inherent accepted level of risk in business, so understand that it is necessary not to be overzealous, but rather, prudent. This is by no means a political statement advocating for more or less regulation in business. There should be a healthy balance between doing what is right and operating as needed to achieve business goals.

Do not fear sharing performance of the business with employees. You are not giving away state secrets or anything proprietary. They will appreciate the inclusion and will commit to having a greater stake in its success. You never know, with the increased buy-in, one of them may aspire to be your next business manager, so feel free to be generous with the knowledge.

Lastly, be sure to institutionalize the newly improved process or all the effort that went into improving it will be lost. It will be challenging to change the culture, but do not let that sway you from reaping the rewards of applying these methodologies. Depending on the size of your organization, be sure to share the learnings from your process improvement initiative with other areas, even when it appears they do not have a similar processes. At the very least they can be made aware that process improvement is occurring within the entity and that they should be conducting their own efforts. When they do, they can work from the examples they've been provided from your team's efforts. Your findings may trigger parallel applicability.

Training material should reflect any changes that were made from improvements. These changes can include the implementation of quality reviews as well as any new controls established. No experience should be considered a bad one; they all teach us something, even if they tell us what not to do. I'll stress here that Process Improvement should not be a one and done. It should be ongoing. Quarterly or yearly reviews of all processes should be an integral part of the business's daily operations and future plans so that Process Improvement is integrated into the very fiber of you business.

IVAN G. BANNOWSKY

7

Motivation

"Just when the caterpillar thought the world was ending, it
turned into a butterfly."

- Proverb

So, what is motivation? The Merriam-Webster
Dictionary defines motivation as such:

- the act or process of giving someone a reason for
  doing something : the act or process of motivating
  someone

- the condition of being eager to act or work : the
  condition of being motivated

- a force or influence that causes someone to do
  something

How interesting is it that motivation is defined as a
process of giving someone a reason or a process of
motivating someone? What I mean is that, it's not some fairy
dust or a feeling, *per se*, rather, it can be a tangible and
obtainable trait through taking real steps. Synonyms for

motivation include; inspiration, stimulus, enthusiasm, instigation, optimism and ambition, all of which are really about exercising your decision-making muscle. The reason I chose the butterfly quote for this chapter is that you will need patience, just as the caterpillar needed, before he could transform and fly.

Typically, people seek out motivation because they are feeling the opposite, be it de-motivated, demoralized or even depressed. I have found that moments of great adversity can often flower moments of great inspiration just by sheer contrast. I have always attempted to tackle my greatest obstacles head on first, knowing that anything smaller will be gravy, if you will, and that usually those large obstacles are what were weighing most heavily on me. It's okay to feel off track occasionally because, sometimes, it is only then that we can find the right track that we need to be on.

If you are having difficulty identifying what motivates you, then it is time to do some exploration to find out what does. Reading and self-educating are great ways to find what it is you may be passionate about. Find like-minded people that share your belief system, and I don't mean exclusively in a religious sense, rather those who share a similar moral compass and way of thinking as you have so that you can unite your efforts towards a common goal. Inversely, be sure not to allow what others think of you define *you*. You can be whatever you want to be. The only perception of you that should matter is your own. You do you and focus on how you feel, not what you think others may think of you.

Wanting to be motivated is the first step to *becoming* motivated, so if you are at least looking to be motivated then that is certainly a step in the right direction. Becoming motivated is not easy for some and it is not something that becomes a state of presence. It has its ebb and flow. It is possible to take control of your life and make your own destiny if you are willing to work for it and want it bad enough. You have an inherent responsibility to the world as a global citizen to leave it better than the way you found, to leave a positive legacy, and to do your best work which is ultimately your life work.

Occasionally, the opposite of motivation is de-motivation which can be as extreme as feeling depressed. Constantly worrying about things can be very debilitating and counterproductive. Here are a few strategies I use when I find myself on this end of the spectrum.

1) Realize that this is temporary and that this too shall pass. Be patient.

2) Don't expect things to fix themselves or that others will fix

it for you. Only you can make it happen, so what are you waiting for?

3) There is always hope. Realize that things usually have a way of working out, however don't take this as an endorsement for complacency. Be sure to make a plan and take action.

4) Focus on putting one foot in front of the other. Do this and eventually you will get to where you need to go.

5) When a new day arrives, recognize it and embrace the opportunity to start fresh.

6) Convert the energy of frustration into the energy of determination

7) Create a 'happy place' for you to go internally. Mine is a hammock between two palm trees on a beach, watching the waves crest and listening to Bob Marley's song *Three Little Birds* which repeats several times "Every little thing's gonna be alright."

Don't let these recommendations be a replacement for professional help; however. We, as humans, can always benefit from having a conversation with another, so don't allow any stigmas regarding mental health deter you from seeking this out. You will be the better for it. That being said, don't allow yourself to be distracted by influences not conducive to your achieving your goals. Don't even make time for that; only make time for what is going to move you forward. Make no mistake; motivation is work. If it were easy, everyone would be motivated, but if you have a plan, you can make it happen. Remember that from chaos, order must rise; from confusion, clarity is born; and from demoralization, comes motivation.

Another great way to find sources of motivation is to tap into your background and your identity. Victory is so much sweeter when you are the underdog. If you come from humble beginnings, like I did, then use that to fuel your ambition to get out of that situation or to ensure you never have to go back to it.

I was born with a severe hearing impairment and have had to wear hearing aids since I was five years old. I can't begin to tell you how much the other kids would torment me and how much those experiences affected me for the longest time. In adulthood; however, I work hard to overcome this disability and to be accepted as an equal even though I do still have challenges. So, I focus on my strengths and find ways to exhibit them as my brand and not dwell on my shortcomings. Do a self-assessment of yourself and find out what it is that you're good at. Ask colleagues to weigh in and provide feedback, be it positive or constructive.

Another strategy for finding motivation is to ask yourself what regrets you might have on your last day of life. I know this is not everyone's favorite subject and it borders on the morbid, however it certainly helps to put things in perspective. Ask yourself, did I truly strive to reach my full potential and did I inspire others along the way. Did I create something, come up with new ideas to make the world a better place, or blaze a trail that others could follow? While there is much that I personally would still like to do in this life, for the most part I am content with what I have accomplished as well as the impact that I've had on those around me. However, I will reiterate; there is still much I would like to do. Leaving a lasting legacy by which to be remembered should be part of your inspiration.

If you do see or think of something that inspires you, be sure to write it down or capture it in some way so that you can retain it instead of attempting to make a mental note of it and run the risk of forgetting it or worse never fulfilling it. This will help reinforce the inspiration and allow you to call on it when you need to take action. This is an exercise that will take practice; however, I can assure you that if you are looking to rewire yourself for motivation this method is imperative. It will be hard in the short term but will become second nature before you know it and you will want to seize the momentum when it happens. There is no expectation that this will be a massive one-time overhaul; rather, it will be a gradual evolution towards a greater sense of empowerment.

Your outlook will be a self-fulfilling prophecy. If you believe that what you are attempting to achieve is either impossible or possible, you will be right on both accounts. So, if you have dreams and you continue to view them as such then they will always be dreams. I'll reiterate here that it is important to define unassailable goals and to develop specific tangible steps to get to those goals. This could include creating a set of well-documented instructions for yourself with specific timelines for when steps need to be completed. What is your goal specifically? What do you see when you visualize yourself reaching that goal? What does it feel, smell, or sound like? Don't forget to reward yourself at each milestone.

The last strategy that I'll touch on for finding motivation is to put things in perspective. There are millions of people on this planet who have a very difficult life. Anytime I start to feel sorry for myself or think that I am somehow entitled to more, I start to think of those that may have no food or shelter and I immediately have a greater appreciation for all that I have. Volunteering in your community is an excellent way to help others less fortunate and you will feel productive in creating more positive energy in the lives of others. I am a firm believer in paying it forward without any expectation of reward other than a satisfaction that I have done at least something to make someone else's day just a little brighter.

Index

Figures Reference

Figures Reference Continued

Thank you for reading!

IVAN G. BANNOWSKY

IVAN G. BANNOWSKY